A Cute Van

by Kelsey Quinn
illustrated by Audrey Durney

Practice Decodable 26

McGraw Hill Education

Bothell, WA • Chicago, IL • Columbus, OH • New York, NY

MHEonline.com

Send all inquiries to:
McGraw-Hill Education
8787 Orion Place
Columbus, OH 43240

ISBN: 978-0-02-144728-2
MHID: 0-02-144728-4

Printed in China.

8 9 10 11 12 DSS 27 26 25 24 23

Not a Bus—Just Vans

Vans were in a line.

Can we find Dad?

Some vans have cubs.
Some vans have cats.

Vans held silk flags.
The flags were big.
Some vans held big quilts.

Take a Look

Then we spot a cute van.
It looks like a cube.

Looks Like Us

But then we find Dad.

His van is the best.

It has us on it!

We jump in!